WHAT HAPPENS WHEN FOOD BURNS?

by India James

Ideas for Parents and Teachers

Pogo Books let children practice reading informational text while introducing them to nonfiction features such as headings, labels, sidebars, maps, and diagrams, as well as a table of contents, glossary, and index.

Carefully leveled text with a strong photo match offers early fluent readers the support they need to succeed.

Before Reading

- "Walk" through the book and point out the various nonfiction features. Ask the student what purpose each feature serves.
- Look at the glossary together. Read and discuss the words.

During Reading

- Have the child read the book independently.
- Invite them to list questions that arise from reading.

After Reading

- Discuss the child's questions. Talk about how they might find answers to those questions.
- Prompt the child to think more. Ask: Have you ever burned food? How did it change the food's flavor?

Pogo Books are published by Jump!
3500 American Blvd W, Suite 150
Bloomington, MN 55431
www.jumplibrary.com

Jump! is a division of FlutterBee Education Group.

Library of Congress Cataloging-in-Publication Data is available at www.loc.gov or upon request from the publisher.

ISBN: 979-8-89213-840-6 (hardcover)
ISBN: 979-8-89213-841-3 (paperback)
ISBN: 979-8-89213-842-0 (ebook)

Editor: Katie Chanez
Designer: Anna Peterson

Photo Credits: dlerick/iStock, cover (foreground); photodeedooo/iStock, cover (background); PeteMuller/iStock, 1; Dio5050/Dreamstime, 3; mphillips007/iStock, 4; AlexRaths/iStock, 5; Pixel-Shot/Shutterstock, 6; gsagi/iStock, 7; BuyMorePlease/Shutterstock, 8–9; charnsitr/Shutterstock, 10–11; hlphoto/Shutterstock, 12–13; Rubberball/Erik Isakson/Getty, 14–15; pamungkas789/Shutterstock, 16–17; Diane Labombarbe/iStock, 18 (recipe card); Mariyana M/Shutterstock, 18 (ingredients); New Africa/Shutterstock, 19 (top), 21 (top); brizmaker/iStock, 19 (bottom); Anna and Vada Peterson, 20–21; Lev Kropotov/Shutterstock, 20 (timer); AWEvans/iStock, 21 (bottom); Zhuravlev Andrey/Shutterstock, 23.

Printed in the United States of America at Corporate Graphics in North Mankato, Minnesota.

TABLE OF CONTENTS

CHAPTER 1

WHAT'S THAT SMELL?

Dinner is cooking. It smells delicious. Then something changes. The food smokes. It turns black. It is burning!

We cook food for many reasons. Food tastes good when it is cooked. Cooking also kills **bacteria** that can make us sick. But sometimes food burns. How? Let's find out!

CHAPTER 2

BURNING BASICS

We heat food to cook it. One way is to cook food over flames or another heat source. Another way is to use hot air. This is how ovens work.

When food cooks at a high temperature, water in the food **evaporates**. Then sugars in the food **react** with **proteins**. The food turns brown. Its **flavor** and smell also change.

If food cooks for too long or gets too hot, it can lead to **combustion**. The heated food reacts with **oxygen** in the air. Flames and smoke may come off the food.

flames

Smoke is made up of gases, water **vapor**, and small **particles** left over from combustion. These particles are what give burning food its smell.

DID YOU KNOW?

Large amounts of cooking smoke can be harmful to your health. If your food smokes, turn on fans or open windows.

As food begins to burn, its proteins and sugars break down. **Molecules** in the food are left behind. They are made of **carbon**. They are the hard, black parts on the food. These are the burnt parts!

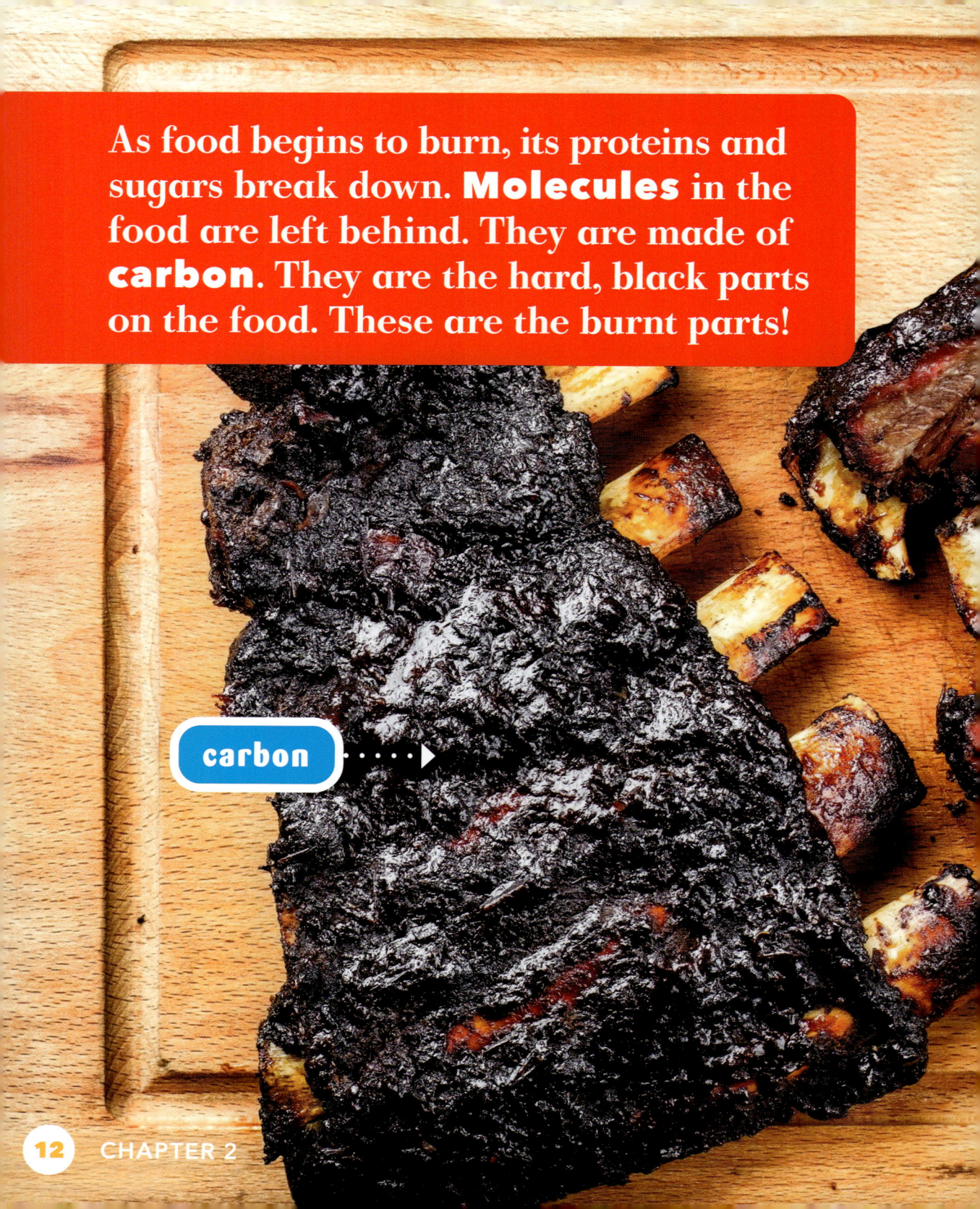

carbon

TAKE A LOOK!

How does food burn? Take a look!

1 Food is heated.

HEAT SOURCE

2 Proteins and sugars react. The food starts to turn brown.

3 When cooked too hot or too long, the food and oxygen combust. Flames and smoke form.

4 Proteins and sugars break down. Carbon is left. The food is burnt.

Burnt food tastes bitter. It can be **inedible**. Sometimes burnt parts can be scraped or cut off. Paying careful attention helps prevent burning. So does using low heat.

char ····▶

Sometimes people burn food on purpose. This turns part of the food black. This is called **charring**. Charring food changes its flavor. A little bitterness can mix well with other flavors!

DID YOU KNOW?

People char many types of food. Meats and vegetables are often charred on a grill. Some chefs char vegetables like peppers on the stove!

CHAPTER 3

LET'S COOK!

Let's make a s'more to see how heat changes a food's color. Ask an adult for help.

S'MORE

INGREDIENTS
marshmallow
graham cracker
chocolate bar

KITCHEN TOOLS
stove
roasting stick
plate

1

Put the marshmallow on the end of the stick.

2

Ask an adult to turn on the stove to low heat.

3

With an adult's help, hold the marshmallow above the burner.

4

Hold it there for 30 seconds. How does it change? What color is it now?

5

Continue to toast the marshmallow until it is as cooked as you like.

6

Snap the graham cracker in half. Set one piece on a plate. Put a piece of chocolate on top. Add the toasted marshmallow. Top it with the other half of the cracker. Enjoy!

ACTIVITIES & TOOLS

TASTING TOAST

Food may taste different the longer it cooks. Find out for yourself as you cook toast. Ask an adult for help.

What You Need:
- toaster
- three slices of bread

❶ **Set the toaster to the lowest cooking level.**

❷ **Put a slice of bread in the toaster. Let it cook. Take it out once it is done.**

❸ **Set the toaster to a medium setting. Put in the second slice of bread. Let it cook. Take it out of the toaster.**

❹ **Set the toaster to the highest setting. Put in the last slice of bread. Let it cook. Then remove it from the toaster.**

❺ **Taste each slice of bread. Do they look, smell, and taste different? Which do you like best?**

GLOSSARY

bacteria: Microscopic, single-celled living things that exist everywhere.

carbon: A chemical element found in all plants and animals.

charring: Slightly burning something.

combustion: The process of bursting into flames and burning.

evaporates: Changes into a gas.

flavor: Taste.

inedible: Not enjoyable to eat.

molecules: The smallest units that chemicals can be divided into.

oxygen: A colorless gas found in air and water that humans and animals need to breathe.

particles: Extremely small pieces of something.

proteins: Nutrients that are found in all living things and are necessary for life.

react: To change chemically by mixing substances together.

vapor: A gas formed from something that is a liquid or solid at normal temperatures.

INDEX

TO LEARN MORE

Finding more information is as easy as 1, 2, 3.

❶ Go to www.factsurfer.com

❷ Enter "foodburns" into the search box.

❸ Choose your book to see a list of websites.

FACT
SURFER